A Primer on Evil

A Primer on Evil

T.

To order additional copies of this book, contact:
Xlibris Corporation
1-888-795-4274
www.Xlibris.com
Orders@Xlibris.com
50037

I dedicate this book to both parents, all four siblings, two old boyfriends and one ex-friend, all of whom taught me how to spot Evil.

I also dedicate it to all the wonderful teachers and professors I've had who taught me to take good notes, organize and categorize, but most of all: write it down!

FORWARD

Primer (prîm-er): a book that covers the basic elements of a subject.

I don't know why a person decides to become Evil, but when they do, they have decided, in effect, to stop growing. The Evil abdicate their responsibility to think, to feel, to *care* about anyone but themselves. All discipline is thrown out the window, and they no longer reign themselves in. They cease to be a burden to themselves any longer, and become instead an enormous burden to everyone around them.

They don't stop controlling; rather, they turn from controlling themselves to controlling others.

Evil is knowable, predictable, and preventable. (That is to say, you can prevent it from affecting your life). Understanding and spotting it is simple. *You just have to stop making excuses for what you're seeing.* The Evil do everything in their power to confuse you and hide. Attributing evil acts to thoughtlessness, addiction, (certain types of) mental illness or old age only assists them in their disguise, but it's just smoke and mirrors. Once you see through it—learn to recognize it for what it is—it's simple.

That's why this book is so short. Each concept is kept as brief as possible so you can remember it and refer to it. A longer, more detailed discussion of Evil makes the subject seem more abstract and theoretical. It's not. It's a part of our lives, and this primer is your first step in combating it.

What is Evil, anyway?

1) The essence of Evil is the deep-seated need
to control others.

2) The Evil abdicate their responsibility to think, to feel, to care about anyone but themselves. All discipline is thrown out the window, and they no longer reign themselves in.*

---

*   They do this for one simple, elegant reason: to get their own way.

What are their traits?

3) The two dominant traits of the Truly Evil are self-righteousness, and self-pity.*

* **All** their actions are justified, and they—The Evil—are the true victims.

4) Evil people have no boundaries. None.

5) They are completely unaware of the pain felt by others.

6) Evil people have a sense of entitlement.
They feel they never have to earn anything.

7) The Evil demand high praise for doing what is expected of them (e.g. honoring promises, dressing appropriately, or providing food for their small children).*

---

*   Since this behavior is hit-or-miss, it explains their bizarre attitude. If they don't receive massive, ongoing praise for each little thing, they simply stop doing it.

T.

How do they live with themselves?

8) The Evil are absolutely convinced of their own lovability.*

* Unlike the rest of us, they need no outside confirmation.

9) The Evil always blame the victim for their own actions.*

---

*   "It's your fault," "You made me do it," "You know you want it," etc. Child molesters are particularly adept at this.

10) Projection rules their world.*

* Evil people project all their traits outward. Liars think you lie, cheaters think you cheat, thieves think you steal. While The Evil feel there is nothing wrong with being liars, cheaters and thieves, any trait considered "unfortunate" by society is rationalized by saying, "You're that way, too."

Where will I tend to find Evil People?

11) Everywhere. But, generally speaking,
The Evil always manage to wedge
themselves into a position of power, stopping
all flow of information and progress.

(What a friend called, "A bung in the asshole of
life.") It is *not* your imagination that the Evil
are drawn to becoming a boss or supervisor.*

---

* They also wedge themselves into smaller positions when they are
particularly low on the social scale: landlords, tow-truck drivers,
your waitress. Power is power. They don't need to destroy a
country when they can destroy you.

12) A "natural" position of power is as a parent,
or in-law. It is used to destroy the children, or
anyone who tries to marry the children.

But, I'm a *nice* person! How does this affect me?

13) Evil preys more easily upon a person's virtues than his vices. This is why a "good" person will twist himself into a pretzel trying to please an Evil person.

You're wrong! I'll "Kill them with kindness."

14) *All* kindness is viewed as weakness.*

*   Don't be an ass. It only shows them how weak (and therefore stupid) you are. Every time you are nice to an Evil Person you reinforce their two core beliefs: 1) Their behavior is perfectly acceptable, and 2) You enjoy their behavior. (You rewarded them when they treated you badly, didn't you? Didn't you?)†

†   If you still don't get it, try this: Your dog craps on your carpet. You reward him with a doggie treat, and clean up the mess. The same thing happens the next day. You reward him and clean up after him. What connection has the dog made in his head? You like it. You like people coming into your home and treating you badly. You reward bad behavior every time you buy evil people a wonderful gift at Christmas, drive them around town or run errands for them. The analogy of cleaning up the dog's mess? You didn't say anything! You didn't speak up and berate the Evil Person for bad behavior, because 1) you're not comfortable believing in evil and 2) you're going to "kill them with kindness."

I'll *earn* their respect by not sinking to their level.

15) Once The Evil view you as a patsy, they will never respect you, no matter what you accomplish. They will view you as a patsy (forever) if you give in to their wishes (once).

Why won't this work? I mean, eventually?

16) The Evil will never be pleased. If The Evil allowed himself or herself to be pleased— even for a second—the game would be over, and the entire point of the game is to play the game. Forever.*

---

* I want to be pleased. You want to be pleased. We even seek out those objects, persons or events that please us. That's normal behavior.

The Evil aren't like that. They willfully and deliberately want to be displeased *all the time.* This (paradoxically) brings them pleasure. Why? **Because it keeps you confused, unhappy and guessing.**

Let's say you are a battered wife. Nothing you do is right, right? Everything you do is wrong, because *the whole point of the game* is to fly into a rage every time you do something wrong. And everything you do is wrong because he shifts the finish line every time you reach it.

He wants to be displeased so he can control you.

Or, you're an adult child trying to please his mother. You leave your wife to go run errands for your mother, fix up her house, loan her money, and still she's never pleased. Why is that? Because the game is rigged.

She wants to be displeased so she can control you.

Or, you try so hard to please your mother-in-law. You buy her nice gifts—thoughtfully wrapped—for Christmas, you change vacation plans because she scheduled her surgery for that time, you take care of her cats even though you are allergic to cats, and yet she's never pleased.

*The whole point of the game is to **play the game.***

17) When we (the good) play this game for years, never winning, we despair, and when we despair we don't choose well. Thus, the game goes on. Forever.

18) In order to play the game forever,
The Evil create the artificial shortage.*

---

*   "If you leave me, no one will ever love you."
    "If you tell anyone about Daddy, they'll come and take me away."

When an Evil person threatens you with abandonment, they're playing a card they don't have. Truly, they'll never abandon you; you should be so lucky.

When a battered wife finally tries to legally sever all ties with her husband, he shoots her at the courthouse.

When a parent says, "Don't darken my doorstep again," as soon as they need money or grow ill, they'll be knocking on your door.

Okay. I'm ready to believe there is Evil in the world.

Other than the obvious, what traits do I look for?

19) The Evil find out what you want, and then take it away from you.*

* This could be as simple as asking you what you'd like for your birthday, and then getting you something completely different.

Remember: The Evil don't really want what you have . . . they simply don't want you enjoying it. Most likely they'll destroy or abandon whatever it is as soon as they take it away from you.

If your sister sleeps with your husband—*out of all the men in the world*—it's not because she wants him, it's because *you* want him.

20) You know them by their gifts.*

*   Everyone, including yourself, has given bizarre or inappropriate gifts at one time or another. Only the Truly Evil do something this strange: They give you something *that is already yours.*

I don't mean something *similar to* something you already own. I mean: they may go into your house, take something off your shelf, wrap it up, and present it to you . . . *as a gift.* (Or go to one of your yard sales, buy something, and present it to you later). They make no pretense that the item wasn't yours to begin with.

Some literal examples: You loan someone a book, and later they present it to you as a gift, not as returning the book. Or they give you some item that you gave them as a gift years before, saying, "You really seemed to enjoy this." Or they borrow money, then, years later, present it as a gift, not as repayment of a loan.

A figurative "gift," (and classic scenario), is the man who beats his wife. He threatens to kill her if everything isn't done his way, if she refuses to have violent sex with him, etc. He is, in essence, saying, "Today, I will *give you your life*, if you do everything just the way I tell you." It's not his to give. Your life is yours *by virtue of being born.*

21) All interactions with the Truly Evil are a series of rewards and punishments.*

* *All of them.* Nothing is benign, nothing is casual.
  When they talk to you, they are gathering information to be used against you. When they give you a gift, it is to put you in their debt. When they withhold affection, show up late, or destroy your property, it is to punish you for not giving in to their wishes.

22) The Evil are often paranoid.
(They're terrified you'll leave). Paranoia is
projection looped back on itself.

Paranoia is projection looped back on itself.

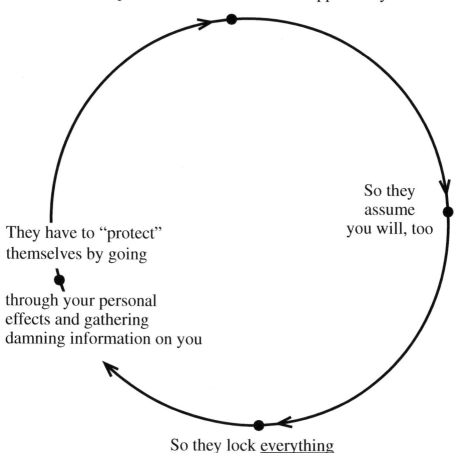

They know <u>they</u> will go through your
personal effects at the least opportunity

So they
assume
you will, too

They have to "protect"
themselves by going

through your personal
effects and gathering
damning information on you

So they lock <u>everything</u>

23) Contrary to widely held belief: The Evil don't really understand (or value) money.*

---

*   Since they only value control, nothing else has any value. When they come to understand that other people value money, then they value controlling it.

24) The Evil have only two motivations: doing that which looks good, and doing that which feels good.*

---

*   Think about it. Good people have all kinds of motivations, which we recognize manifestly as being normal: to live well, to die in peace surrounded by loved ones, to marry (or not) so as to connect with another, to have many friends (or one good one), to have children (or not), to leave a legacy, to be productive. And finally: to be recognized and rewarded for that productiveness.

Evil people marry in order to appear normal (to "look good"), and to abuse and slowly destroy their spouse ("do bad"). They have children to appear normal ("looking good"), and to rape, beat or verbally abuse those children ("doing bad"). They work, eat and pay rent so that they have the energy and sanctuary with which to commit those acts; not because they care about good food and a nice house.

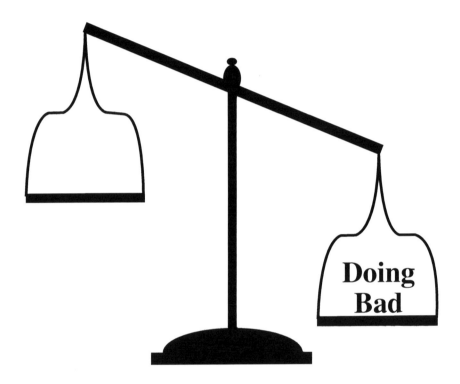

When they think no one is looking.

When they know someone is looking.

I know someone who is Evil. What does the future hold?

25) By fifty, you get the face you deserve.*

* The façade of niceness that The Evil can affect when they are in their 20's and 30's begins to crumble when they age. It requires enormous energy to maintain a "nice" face.

They also grow tired and angry of even the pretense of niceness. Thus, they will quit their jobs, get rid of all their friends and stop paying mortgage or rent, so that they can sponge off of you and not have to even "pretend" to be nice anymore. This is the best of all possible worlds to the Truly Evil.

26) "The meaner you are, the longer God lets you live."*

---

*   The reason The Evil live so long and have so few (real) illnesses is that they are no longer a burden to themselves; rather, they are a burden to others. Stress is probably the number one killer in first-world countries: the cumulative effects will kill you. The Evil suffer no such ill effects.

Where do I stand?

27) All Evil people are control freaks;
not all control freaks are Evil.
There is a difference in kind, and degree.

28) On a scale of controlling others:
The opposite of good is bad.
The opposite of Evil is Holy.*

* *Nothing, and no one, is neutral.* If you're not part of the solution
(fighting Evil at every opportunity) you're part of the problem:
you contribute to Evil behavior by saying, and doing, nothing.
(Or—worse yet—doing them favors and buying them gifts).

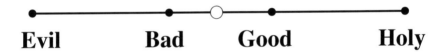

Evil   **Bad**   **Good**   **Holy**

<u>No</u>
self control.
All energy is
put into
controlling
others.

Exercise
<u>extreme</u>
self-control:
Jesus
Buddha
Gandhi
et al.

Is there hope for The Evil?

29) No. The Evil will never become good.*

---

*   They don't see the benefit. There is no easily discernable payoff for them. Also, their fear of letting go of even *one ounce* of control is too great.

What can I do to protect myself?

30) Exercise restraint and authority (control).
The Evil are obedient to power.*

---

* Wife beaters are compliant in the custody of police and in front
of juries. Evil managers are submissive when the president of the
company is around.

How do I get control?

31) You NEVER ask for control from an Evil Person; they won't give it. You take it from them. (Your weapons for doing so are in the back of the book).

Won't that be "controlling others?" Won't that make *me* Truly Evil?

32) No. Think of it as teaching your dog
(boss, mother-in-law, spouse) not to crap on
the carpet. You're making the
world a better place.

Is there any sort of "scratch test" to determine if a person is Evil?

33) Sure; the nicer you are,
the meaner they get.
Works every time.

Last, but never least . . .

34) The single most fascinating fact about Good vs. Evil . . . *

* The single most fascinating (and truly disheartening) fact about Good vs. Evil is that *each group*, in their heart of hearts and soul of souls, doesn't believe the other group exists.

I've just given ample examples of The Good not really believing Evil exists. The Evil, for their part, have no word for The Good. They *never* refer to good people as "good."

Instead, they have a thousand other words: sucker, jerk, moron, asshole, bitch, bait, cunt, mark . . . ad nauseum.

This is how they rationalize their behavior. This is how they *see* you: not as a good person, but as a patsy. I hope you use that information to stop being nice to Evil People, and start controlling (putting a limit on) their behavior.

CRIMINAL ACTS

If a crime is (or has been) committed by an Evil Person, call 911.

When my brother recently mentioned that years ago he was involved in a hit-and-run, I turned him in to the cops. I didn't weigh his reaction; I didn't care—I did the right thing.

If you're wondering why he would reveal something so casually, it's because (a) he didn't really think of it as a crime and (b) he didn't think I'd go to the police.

Evil people can *never quite* make the connection between cause and effect. He truly did not believe I would go to the cops, and unfortunately, that's true in most families.

I am absolutely convinced that *every single murder* in the United States could be solved if family members turned in their own. Criminals always brag; they can't help it. It's up to good people—you and me—to turn them in. We are the gatekeepers. Evil People don't police their own actions. (Duh!)

I'm not going to tell you what happened next with my brother because it's irrelevant. **You always do the right thing**, and let the chips fall where they may.

WEAPONS

I assume you've already tried the word, "No." If your experience was like mine, the person became enraged. They either blew up at you, or, more likely, did a slow boil and started making plans to foil you. They pretended not to hear you and started speaking and acting around your attempts to put a stop to their behavior. This is typical.

The word "no" works with good people, and strangers trying to take advantage of you for the first time. The strangers will know you are not an easy mark and go away, and good people will simply say, "Okay," and move on. They will treat you with the same respect they showed you before you said no.

The naiveté in thinking that the word "no" will work with friends and relatives who have cultivated you as a patsy is understandable, but mistaken. *They will never let you go*. The direct approach either enrages them, or they re-write what you said. Remember: evil people are absolutely convinced of their own lovability. When you finally lose it and say, "Look: I don't love you! I don't even *like* you, so go away," there will be a lot of alligator tears, they will go away for awhile, and then they'll come right back and act as if nothing happened.

The only way to get rid of them is to make your company so poisonous and disagreeable, that they finally go away. You'll have to do this more than once, because they don't "get it."

I wouldn't write this book without giving you weapons. You picked up this book because of all the evil people in your life who make you miserable, but who aren't (technically) criminals. Now, I can give you, one by one, dozens of different weapons, but they all fall under the same category, regardless of the evil person, their particular behavior, or their relationship to you: The Truth.

Everything that follows assumes adults are involved. It not only won't work with children, I would never call a child "evil."

Sit down and, *without elaboration*, write down *the exact* word or phrase that describes the person. Practice saying it in a flat (but not robot-like) voice. The Truth, delivered at exactly the right moment, in exactly the proper tone of voice (calm) while looking directly at the offender, is devastating.

I've seen it. I've done it.

The phrase should be no longer than nine words. I'm not kidding. Studies with small children have shown that *they stop hearing you* after nine words. Make no reference to yourself (e.g. "It hurts me when you do that"). It's like pointing a gun to your chest and pulling the trigger. All ammunition is aimed outward in short, perfectly aimed volleys.

Always do it in front of at least one other person. The more witnesses, the better. The more the blow hurts them.

Some deceptively powerful ones: "You're a bully," "You're a control-freak," "You're a tyrant," "You're a narcissist."

Said quietly, in front of witnesses, dropped almost as a non-sequitor, absolutely destroys the other person. Especially if you do it around the holidays. If you *say nothing else*, the person will flip-out. They'll lose it. They'll walk frantically around the room, raising their voice, getting sarcastic, verbally attacking you, your spouse, your children, your shoes. They will never find their footing for the rest of the day.

Be aware that it will come back to you. They will try and punish you a thousand different ways in the year that follows. Just wait, be patient, and *do it again*. Use a different word or phrase. If you called them a control-freak before, call them a little-Hitler this time.

In summation:

1) Wait for the holidays or a family get-together.
2) Wait until they say something nasty, or try to control you.
3) In front of witnesses, say, "You're a tyrant," or similar phrase. Say it quietly.
4) *Say nothing else*. Remain silent; don't rise to any bait.
5) Be prepared for a huge backlash in the months that follow.

Here's *one* of my many examples: My brother-in-law is verbally abusive and emotionally manipulative to my sister-in-law. He avoids me like the plague because he can't push me around. He made the mistake of verbally diminishing my sister-in-law's opinion in front of me. I waited until he was done and said, "You're a bully."

It was electric. He grabbed his son and, saying nothing, walked out of the room. She turned on me like a lioness, and I haven't seen him at family get-togethers for *nine years*, even though they are still married.

All of this is typical. I said the tiniest little phrase, but it was the *exact truth*, and it rocked their world. His reaction was to avoid me. She was vicious to me because I had exposed the dirty little secret of their marriage. I don't care because I don't stand by when men abuse their wives or girlfriends, but you must be mentally and emotionally prepared for the fall-out.

Here's another example: my sister was calling me sly names, implying I was stupid . . . *at Christmas*. I waited until she was partially done (this would have gone on throughout the day), then said, "You're a tyrant and a control-freak," almost as an aside.

It destroyed her world. She was walking back and forth, saying things that didn't make sense, when, abruptly, she decided she had to go the hospital (it was never made clear why). Her point was to give herself cover ("I'm not upset, I'm sick") and to ruin Christmas for everyone else, not to mention draw attention to herself.

Now I'll give you one of the best: "You're not a better person than I am."

Think about it: *of course* they think they're better than you, but there is an injunction in polite societies not to *say* it. Since evil people imagine themselves to be cultured, they can't say, "Of course I am!" Their hands (and tongue) are tied.

So watch—*say nothing*—as they attempt to get around that. So what if they say, "I suppose you think you're better than I am"? C'mon. That's right up there with, "What bounces off of me sticks to you." It carries no weight. Don't smile, don't say anything, and *never turn in battle*. Just stare at them. People don't like silences. They'll go nuts trying to fill the void.

The point is to emit a stink, like a fog, of truth around yourself every time they are near. This is the only thing that works, since the direct approach—putting distance being yourself and the evil person, saying "no," telling them to go away—just doesn't work.

My Notes

My Notes

2965506

Made in the USA